INHERIT
THE WIND

Jerome Lawrence & Robert E. Lee

EDITORIAL DIRECTOR Justin Kestler
EXECUTIVE EDITOR Ben Florman
DIRECTOR OF TECHNOLOGY Tammy Hepps

SERIES EDITORS John Crowther, Justin Kestler
MANAGING EDITOR Vince Janoski

WRITER Christian Lorentzen
EDITOR Matt Blanchard

This edition published by Spark Publishing

Spark Publishing
A Division of SparkNotes LLC
120 Fifth Avenue, 8th Floor
New York, NY 10011

First edition.

Please submit all comments and questions or report errors to www.sparknotes.com/errors

Library of Congress Catalog-in-Publication Data available upon request

Printed and bound in the United States

ISBN 1-58663-829-7

INTRODUCTION:
STOPPING TO BUY SPARKNOTES ON A SNOWY EVENING

Whose words these are you *think* you know.
Your paper's due tomorrow, though;
We're glad to see you stopping here
To get some help before you go.

Lost your course? You'll find it here.
Face tests and essays without fear.
Between the words, good grades at stake:
Get great results throughout the year.

Once school bells caused your heart to quake
As teachers circled each mistake.
Use SparkNotes and no longer weep,
Ace every single test you take.

Yes, books are lovely, dark, and deep,
But only what you grasp you keep,
With hours to go before you sleep,
With hours to go before you sleep.

CONTENTS

CONTEXT

HARLES DARWIN'S THEORY OF EVOLUTION was one of the most revolutionary scientific ideas to emerge during the nineteenth century. The theory, which Darwin developed in his landmark work *On the Origin of Species* (1859), proposes that the living organisms found on the Earth today evolved from simpler organisms in a long, gradual process of natural selection. In short, the natural environment favors, or selects, organisms that are best adapted to survive in that environment. Those organisms that are not well adapted to the environment struggle and eventually become extinct.

Darwin's theory caused great controversy because it challenged existing ideas about the origins of humankind, such as the creation story told in the book of Genesis in the Bible. This controversy divided America, which was going through great social change during the period in which Darwin's theories became widespread. Industrialization, urbanization, long-distance transportation, increased access to education, and wave after wave of immigration transformed the United States from a country composed largely of backwater territories into a modern, egalitarian nation. In large cities, particularly on the East Coast, Americans quickly embraced new ideas, values, and technologies. Many regions of the country, however, particularly the South and the Midwest, were slow to sacrifice traditional beliefs.

Two camps formed in response to Darwin. Evolutionists eagerly accepted Darwin's ideas and believed that humans shared a relatively close common ancestor with apes and other primates. Creationists, meanwhile, firmly believed in the literal truth of the creation story in the Bible, which claims that humans appeared on Earth fully formed. The debate between evolutionists and creationists raged throughout the late nineteenth and early twentieth centuries.

Inherit the Wind recounts the famous 1925 criminal trial *Tennessee v. John Thomas Scopes* (often referred to as the "Scopes Monkey Trial"), which was a landmark in the debate between evolutionists and creationists. In 1922, John Washington Butler, a Tennessee legislator, had argued that the Bible provided the basis for the American governmental system and that therefore any deviance from the Bible constituted disrespect for the law. During his second term in the Tennessee legislature, Butler penned the Butler Act, which prohibited the teaching of evolution in Tennessee public schools. The Tennessee legislature passed the law by a wide margin, and in 1925 the governor signed the act into law.

The American Civil Liberties Union (ACLU), based in New York City, opposed the Butler Act and others like it that were springing up in other states. They sought a teacher willing to challenge the law and offered to cover all of that teacher's trial expenses. A businessman named George Rappleyea from Dayton, Tennessee, saw the ACLU's appeal and regarded it as a potential economic opportunity for his impoverished county. After consulting with local leaders and obtaining their consent, Rappleyea recruited John Scopes, a twenty-four-year-old substitute science teacher. Scopes agreed to challenge the Butler Act in the classroom. He taught Darwin's theory to his classes, and in the summer of 1925, the town constable arrested him.

The American media took immediate interest in the Scopes trial and sent reporters to cover it, most notably the muckraking critic H. L. Mencken of the *Baltimore Sun*. Both sides recognized that the Scopes trial would be a highly significant opening battle in an ideological war between progressives and fundamentalists over freedom of thought. Conservatives recruited William Jennings Bryan, one of the most prominent figures in American Christian fundamentalism, to serve as prosecuting attorney. Bryan's lengthy résumé in public service included two terms as a U.S. congressman, a post as secretary of state under President Woodrow Wilson, and three unsuccessful campaigns for the U.S. presidency. To counter Bryan, the prominent criminal litigator Clarence Darrow, an avowed agnostic, volunteered as Scopes's defense attorney.

Scopes's trial provided some intense courtroom drama. Early in the trial, the defense tried to call several experts on evolutionary theory to the witness stand, but the judge ruled this testimony inadmissible. After that ruling, the media believed that the defense had been painted into a corner, with no possible effective strategies left. Darrow, the defense attorney, made a dramatic and unexpected move by calling to the stand the prosecutor, Bryan, as an expert witness on matters relating to the Bible. Darrow's line of questioning forced Bryan to admit that his own literal interpretation of the Bible—a basic tenet of Christian fundamentalism—was full of contradictions. Darrow's questioning prompted many courtroom spectators to shift their support to the defense.

The following day, the judge ordered that Bryan's testimony be stricken from the record, resulting in a guilty verdict for Scopes and a victory for Bryan. However, Darrow and Scopes, through press coverage of the trial and popular support for the defense, won a moral victory that reflected the changing times. Bryan died in his sleep five days after the trial's conclusion. Scopes was acquitted on a technicality in a higher court of appeals.

In the early 1950s, playwrights Jerome Lawrence and Robert E. Lee adapted the Scopes trial into a play. The work, *Inherit the Wind*, was first performed in New York in 1955. Although the playwrights took creative liberties with the story, their version, which draws heavily from journalist H. L. Mencken's coverage of the trial, is true to the spirit of the trial and to the characters of its most prominent players. Lawrence and Lee, who had collaborated since the late 1940s, went on to write more than thirty works together before Lee's death in 1994.

Although the Scopes trial was a dramatic high point in the debate between evolutionists and creationists, the trial failed to resolve the constitutionality of the Butler Act, which remained a Tennessee state law until 1967. Since that time, mainstream America has largely accepted evolution theory as an essential part of basic science education. However, similar issues involving the separation between church and state continue to play a part in legal controversies—for example, school prayer and religious education in public schools, among many others—to this day.

PLOT OVERVIEW

T THE COURTHOUSE IN HILLSBORO, a small Southern town, Bertram Cates is behind bars, awaiting trial for teaching his students about Darwin's theory of evolution. Rachel Brown, a friend and fellow teacher who also is the daughter of the town's minister, visits Cates. She brings Cates some clean clothes and urges him to plead guilty and throw himself at the mercy of the court. Cates remains firm in his resolve.

Hillsboro erupts with excitement as prominent lawyers and journalists arrive for the trial. E. K. Hornbeck, a critic for the *Baltimore Herald*, surveys the scene and makes wisecracks. The Bible-thumping politician Matthew Harrison Brady, who leads the prosecution, arrives to a warm welcome from the townspeople and a picnic in his honor. Brady meets with Reverend Brown, District Attorney Tom Davenport, and the mayor. Brady also holds a confidential discussion with Rachel about her friendship with Cates. Rachel leaves the discussion feeling that she has betrayed her friend.

Hornbeck informs the crowd that the prominent litigator Henry Drummond will represent the defense. The mayor names Brady an honorary colonel in the state militia. Reverend Brown and the mayor discuss how they might prevent Drummond from entering Hillsboro. When the crowd disperses, Rachel and Hornbeck discuss Hornbeck's columns, which portray Cates as a hero. Around sunset, Hornbeck greets Drummond, who has just arrived in town.

A few days later, Drummond, Brady, Davenport, and the judge conduct jury selection. They accept the illiterate Mr. Bannister. Brady makes a joke about Drummond's bright purple suspenders, but Drummond turns the tables by revealing that he bought the suspenders in Brady's Nebraska hometown. As jury selection continues, Brady rejects Mr. Dunlap, a fervent supporter of Brady. Drummond mockingly objects to Brady's honorary title of "colonel," so the judge grants Drummond the same title to even the score. Brady and Drummond accept Sillers, a feed store employee, as a juror. Drummond, who argues that the evolutionist movement should be given the same amount of attention as the fundamentalist movement, notes that the townspeople have erected a sign commanding "Read Your Bible!" in the town square and have advertised prayer meetings. Frustrated by Drummond's demands, the judge declares the court in recess.

A crowd of admirers surrounds Brady as he leaves the courtroom, but no one dares to come near Drummond. Before Drummond leaves the courtroom, Rachel expresses to him her concerns about the trial. Cates relates the hardships he has endured since his arrest. Drummond, who empathizes with Cates's struggle and isolation, offers Cates the opportunity to change his plea on one condition: that Cates truly believes he has done wrong. Cates decides to persevere for his cause. Rachel, however, informs them that Brady has asked her to testify against Cates. A frantic Cates returns to his cell, concerned about the details of personal conversations that Rachel might betray. Drummond reassures Rachel that Brady is less powerful than she believes. Assuring her that Cates is fighting for a worthy cause, Drummond compliments Rachel on her strength in loving Cates.

On the courthouse lawn, Brady leads a group of reporters to a prayer meeting that Reverend Brown is about to conduct. Brady tells the reporters about his former friendship with Drummond. Brown begins the prayer meeting with a quick recitation of the creation story presented in Genesis. He proceeds to incite the crowd into a frenzy. The climax of Reverend Brown's rant is an incantation to bring the fires of hell down on Cates. When Rachel protests, her father requests the same curse for her. Brady, disturbed by Brown's zeal, interrupts and reminds the preacher of the Christian doctrine of forgiveness. Brady calls the prayer meeting to an end and then speaks to Drummond about their old ties and how they have drifted apart.

Two days later, in the courtroom, Brady questions thirteen-year-old Howard Blair about Cates's teaching. Howard confirms that Cates taught him that humans descended from "Old World Monkeys" and that his teachings on creation omitted any reference to God. Cross-examining Howard, Drummond asks the boy about evolutionary theory. The prosecution objects, but Drummond claims he is trying to establish the basic human right to think. The prosecution and the judge counter that the trial is not about the right to think. Drummond asks Howard whether evolutionary theory has harmed him, and the question confuses the boy. Drummond asks Howard if he believes what Cates taught him. Howard says he hasn't made up his mind. Drummond then asks the boy what he thinks of modern technological advances that are not mentioned in the Bible. Howard is again confused, and Brady objects. Drummond rails against Brady's absolute notions of right and wrong. Drummond asks Howard if he understands what is being discussed. When the boy says no, he is dismissed.

The prosecution calls Rachel to the stand. To explain why Cates stopped attending church, Rachel tells the story of Tommy Stebbins. An intellectually curious boy, Stebbins was one of Cates's favorite students. When Stebbins drowned in a local river, Rachel's father preached that the boy would suffer eternal damnation because his parents never had him baptized. Upset both by the death of the boy and the preacher's reaction, Cates stopped going to church. Brady asks Rachel further questions about her discussion of Cates's ideas, but Rachel falters and becomes visibly upset. The prosecution rests its case.

Drummond attempts to call several expert scientists to testify about evolutionary theory, but the judge says that their testimony is inadmissible. Drummond shifts gears and calls Brady to the stand as an expert on the Bible. Asking Brady several questions about Biblical passages that defy the tenets of modern science, Drummond catches Brady off balance and gains the support of the crowd. As Drummond exposes contradiction after contradiction in Brady's views, Brady becomes hysterical and begins to shout names from the Bible. Davenport objects, and the judge adjourns the court.

The next day, just before the jury reads its verdict, Cates and Drummond discuss Cates's chances. A radio reporter enters the courtroom to set up his equipment. The mayor takes the judge aside and tells him that political forces in the state are growing worried about media coverage of the trial. The mayor implicitly tells the judge to pass a light sentence. The jury hands their verdict to the judge, who declares Cates guilty and fines him $100. The prosecution objects to the light sentence. Drummond demands an appeal, and the judge grants him thirty days to prepare it.

The judge adjourns the court. Brady tries to read some prepared remarks, but the spectators in the courtroom begin to leave. Brady tries to deliver the speech to the radio reporter, but the reporter says that the station producer has cut him off. Brady has a mental breakdown and must be carried out of the courtroom as he deliriously recites what sounds like a presidential campaign victory speech. Hornbeck mocks Brady, while Cates expresses concern for him.

Meeker, the bailiff, tells Cates that Hornbeck and the *Baltimore Herald* have posted $500 for Cates's bail. Rachel tells Cates that she has decided to leave her father and that she has overcome her fear of thinking for herself. Word arrives that Brady has died of a "busted belly," and Cates, Rachel, and Drummond decide to leave together on the train out of town that evening.

CHARACTER LIST

Bertram Cates A twenty-four-year-old science teacher and the defendant in the trial. A soft-spoken and humble man, Cates has been arrested for teaching his students the theory of evolution from a biology textbook. His outlook on human knowledge is skeptical, and he wonders about the nature of the universe.

Matthew Harrison Brady A national political figure and a three-time loser in presidential campaigns who arrives in Hillsboro to lead the prosecution in Cates's trial. A Christian fundamentalist and Nebraska native, Brady defends the literal truth of the Bible against what he labels Cates's big-city agnosticism. Drummond, however, exposes the obvious contradictions of this viewpoint, much to Brady's embarrassment.

Henry Drummond A famous lawyer from Chicago whom the *Baltimore Herald* sends to defend Cates. Drummond, a believer in human progress, argues for freedom of thought.

E. K. Hornbeck A cynical, wisecracking journalist and critic who speaks in colorful phrases. Hornbeck travels to Hillsboro to cover the trial for the *Baltimore Herald*. He despises Brady's religious fundamentalism and the townspeople's simple-minded acceptance of Brady's views. In his column, Hornbeck portrays Cates as a hero.

Rev. Jeremiah Brown The figure of religious authority in Hillsboro. Reverend Brown preaches a creed based on the fear of God and the punishment of sinners.

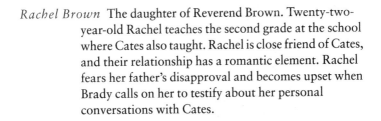

Rachel Brown The daughter of Reverend Brown. Twenty-two-year-old Rachel teaches the second grade at the school where Cates also taught. Rachel is close friend of Cates, and their relationship has a romantic element. Rachel fears her father's disapproval and becomes upset when Brady calls on her to testify about her personal conversations with Cates.

The Judge The judge presiding over Cates's trial. The judge conducts the trial impartially, although his personal views about the Bible's legitimacy are in line with those of the rest of the townspeople of Hillsboro. At the mayor's prompting, the judge gives Cates a lenient sentence after the jury's guilty verdict.

Meeker The bailiff at the Hillsboro courthouse. Meeker lets Cates in and out of his jail cell and jokes that Cates is a threat to the community.

Mrs. Brady Matthew Harrison Brady's wife. Mrs. Brady monitors her husband and nags him not to overeat. Brady calls her "Mother."

Melinda Loomis A twelve-year-old girl. Melinda believes in the Bible and fears the idea of evolution.

Howard Blair A student in Cates's science class. Howard grasps the idea of evolution in only a rudimentary way, as we see when he asks a worm in the play's opening scene what it wants to be when it grows up. At the trial, Howard gives testimony that is used against Cates.

Mrs. Krebs An outspoken Hillsboro woman. On behalf of the Hillsboro Ladies' Aid, Mrs. Krebs serves lunch to Brady on his arrival in town.

Tommy Stebbins An eleven-year-old boy who drowned while swimming in a river. Cates befriended Stebbins, who had a curious nature and enjoyed looking through Cates's microscope. According to Reverend Brown,

Stebbins was damned when he died because he was never baptized. Brown's harsh condemnation of Stebbins disgusted Cates, who stopped attending church.

Mr. Bannister A member of the jury. Bannister has read neither Darwin nor the Bible because he is illiterate.

Elijah A mountain man. The illiterate Elijah sells Bibles to the townspeople and preaches his beliefs to the crowd.

Mayor The mayor of Hillsboro. The mayor supports Brady and welcomes him to town by naming him an honorary colonel in the state militia. Under pressure from the state capitol, he instructs the judge to pass a lenient sentence at the trial's conclusion.

Tom Davenport The local district attorney. Davenport assists Brady during the trial. He attempts to stop Drummond's humiliation of Brady at the end of the trial, but by the time he objects, Brady has already made a fool of himself.

Harry Y. Esterbrook A radio host from WGN in Chicago. Esterbrook broadcasts the announcement of the verdict and Cates's sentencing and cuts off Brady in the middle of his victory speech.

Jesse H. Dunlap A farmer and cabinetmaker. Dunlap stands as a potential juror, but Drummond dismisses him because of his enthusiastic support of Brady.

Sillers An employee at the local feed store and a member of the jury. Drummond accepts Sillers as a juror after Sillers tells him that he focuses on making a living while his wife takes care of religious matters for both of them.

Storekeeper The owner of a store across the square from the courthouse. The storekeeper professes not to have convictions about creation because they are not good for business.

ANALYSIS OF MAJOR CHARACTERS

HENRY DRUMMOND

The infamous criminal-defense attorney Henry Drummond arrives in Hillsboro vilified as an atheist but leaves, after losing the trial, as a hero. To the audience—and to many of the townspeople—Drummond makes a convincing case for the right of a human being to think. He accomplishes this feat by exposing the contradictions underlying his witnesses' inherited religious beliefs. During the case, Drummond demonstrates that people know less than what they believe themselves to know. His greatest triumph in the name of free thought is getting Howard Blair to admit that he has not made up his mind about evolutionary theory. When we hear this admission, Drummond's point becomes clear: freedom of thought becomes the freedom to be wrong or to change our minds. The world, viewed in this light, is full of possibilities.

Although Drummond typically exposes the shortcomings of his subjects' beliefs in gentle fashion, his cross-examination of Matthew Harrison Brady causes humiliation and hysteria. Brady self-destructs when his convictions about the literal truth of the Bible wither under the light of Drummond's skepticism. Until that point, Drummond deploys his wry wit—his purple suspenders from Nebraska, his cracks about the unfairness of Brady's title and the judge's announcement of a Bible meeting but no evolutionist meeting—to no one's harm, while ironically exposing the injustice that his defendant faces. While Drummond's attack of Brady is not mean-spirited, it is devastating. At the same time, the power of Drummond's attack stems not so much from Drummond's wit as from the weight of Brady's egotism, stubbornness, and arrogance as they collapse in his ranting testimony.

Unlike Brady, Drummond does not conceive of truth as a set of fixed rules that can be read from a book and imposed on society. His wonder about the world, which he shares and encourages in Cates, allows him to "look behind the paint," to interpret events for more than their obvious meanings. Drummond's thorough examination of his witnesses' beliefs exposes complexities and contradictions in the same way that Cates's microscopes reveal to his students complexities of life and matter not visible to the naked eye.

MATTHEW HARRISON BRADY

At the beginning of *Inherit the Wind*, Brady arrives pompously, confident that the trial is as good as won. Scornful of the threat that Drummond might present to him as the opposing attorney, Brady exhibits hubris, or excessive pride, in failing to consider the prospect of his own humiliation. Playing on his home turf in rural Christian Tennessee, Brady basks in the glow of his simple-minded supporters' praise. When Drummond undermines Brady's authority, Brady breaks down, for he lacks the inner strength to reconsider his own beliefs and adjust to an unexpected challenge.

We learn that Brady ran for president in three consecutive elections but never succeeded. This failure plagues him throughout his life and manifests itself during the trial. When Brady falls ill following his floundering responses to Drummond's line of questioning, he deliriously spews forth the speech he had prepared for a possible presidential victory. Brady is a caricature of the real-life prosecutor William Jennings Bryan. Like Brady, Bryan lost three presidential elections and died shortly after the Scopes Monkey Trial. In *Inherit the Wind*, as in the national media in 1925, Brady's / Bryan's death symbolized the humiliation he suffered in the trial and the end of an obsolete brand of politics. Bryan was a Democrat, but in the decades after his death, his party took on a more progressive, liberal stance. Not that conservative elements disappeared from American politics—they now exist as tenets of the Republican party.

Although his politics and values are rigidly fundamentalist, Brady remains a complex character. Although he subscribes to a rather traditional brand of Christianity, he embraces more of the Bible than the Hillsboro preacher Reverend Brown does. When Brown harshly calls for eternal hellfire as punishment for Cates and all those who side with him—including even his own daughter—Brady interrupts Brown and reminds the crowd of the Christian doctrine of forgiveness. Brown's version of Christianity, with its frequent casting out of sinners, is grounded in the harsher books of the Old Testament. Brady's, on the other hand, recognizes the more compassionate elements of Jesus' message and the possibilities that this compassion creates for mankind.

BERTRAM CATES

As his jailer, Mr. Meeker, points out, Bertram Cates is not a criminal type. A quiet, unassuming twenty-four-year-old, Cates is innocent, naïve, and wondrous about the world—and he suffers emotionally as a result of the townspeople's treatment of him. He struggles to stand up as an individual even as the crowd opposes his views and actions. Although he remains idealistic throughout *Inherit the Wind*, he often needs Drummond's encouragement to persevere with his cause. Cates doubts himself at times, especially when Rachel pleads him to admit his guilt and beg forgiveness.

In several instances in the play, Cates displays the humanity of an open, forgiving mind, as do the other evolutionists and progressives. Ironically, forgiveness comes more readily to Cates than to his staunchly Christian neighbors—foremost among them Reverend Brown, whose fire-and-brimstone sermons led Cates to abandon the church. Although Rachel unwittingly and unwillingly betrays Cates by testifying against him at Brady's behest, he sympathizes with her pain as she becomes distraught during her time on the witness stand. In fact, Cates urges the court to dismiss Rachel from the stand, which denies her the chance to defend Cates when questioned by Drummond. In the end, when Cates leaves town with Rachel, we see that his trial has opened Rachel's mind as well.

RACHEL BROWN

Rachel's romance with Cates runs parallel to her own personal development and highlights the primary conflict in the play—fundamentalism versus freedom of thought. Rachel's budding emotions pull her away from her father, Reverend Brown, the religious leader of Hillsboro. As Rachel tells more of her story, her father and the form of Christianity practiced in Hillsboro appear more and more cruel and heartless. Rachel relates that her father always frightened her, even from a young age. He publicly confirms her fears at a town prayer meeting, when he damns her soul for supporting Cates. As Rachel's romantic interest, Cates, who teaches evolution to his students and brings an open mind to matters of science and religion, stands in bold opposition to Rachel's father and his views. Perhaps most important, Cates refrains from imposing his own views on others and is willing to engage in constant questioning of ideas. Throughout *Inherit the Wind*, these two characters—Cates and Reverend Brown—test Rachel's loyalties. At the conclusion of the trial, Rachel separates from her father and departs with Cates—a choice that enables her personal liberation.

THEMES, MOTIFS & SYMBOLS

THEMES

Themes are the fundamental and often universal ideas explored in a literary work.

FUNDAMENTALISM VS. FREEDOM OF THOUGHT

Although the trial in *Inherit the Wind* concerns the battle between creationism and evolutionism, a deeper conflict exists beneath the surface. Drummond points to this more basic issue when he asks his young witness Howard whether he believes in Darwin. When the boy responds that he hasn't made up his mind, Drummond insists that the boy's freedom to think—to make up his own mind—is what is actually on trial.

The creationists in the play, who adhere to rigid, fundamental Christian doctrines, are a conservative force that has prescribed for Hillsboro society how their minds should be made up. Their conservatism is rooted in fear. The most adamant creationists, Brady and Reverend Brown, occupy positions of authority at the top of the social order, and their primary motivation is to maintain this control over that social order. Like Darwinism, which questions the religious foundation of that social order, new, progressive ideas present a threat to the creationists' status as leaders.

Drummond, Hornbeck, and Cates, though they maintain respectable positions within society—attorney, journalist, and teacher, respectively—are more interested in the truth than in maintaining their own social status. Their willingness to stand by their own judgments even as they call those judgments to question indicates their self-reliance—a trait that is notably absent in Brown and Brady, who lean instead on the legitimacy gained by their status as religious leaders. Brown, for instance, uses fire-and-brimstone sermons to root out dissent in the Hillsboro community and within his own family. The obedience he demands of the community is the opposite of freedom. In contrast, the questioning that Cates practices—and encourages—promotes free thinking, which opens new paths to progress.

THE CITY VS. THE COUNTRY

In the early twentieth century, rapid urbanization, immigration, and technological improvements exposed American city dwellers to a wide range of new ideas. Although advances in transportation and communication enabled these ideas to spread throughout the United States, many rural areas were slow to accept these new ways of thinking.

In *Inherit the Wind*, Hillsboro and its residents exemplify this conservative, rural mindset. Hillsboro's largely static townspeople are seldom exposed to new faces, let alone new ideas. Many are illiterate or have received education solely from a single, conservative perspective—fundamentalist Christianity. Within the small confines of their town, Reverend Brown's parishioners are content and complacent because their day-to-day environment never presents them with any new or contrary ideas.

When the trial starts, Drummond, Hornbeck, the radio announcer, and several prestigious scientists arrive in Hillsboro from the nation's big cities, hoping to teach the locals a lesson in progress and free thought. Brady and Brown, meanwhile, cast Drummond as the devil, an agnostic crawling from the city gutters to defile the purity of Hillsboro's citizens. The gruff manners of Drummond and Hornbeck do little to endear them to their new small-town acquaintances. In contrast, Brady, though a figure of national prominence, showboats his humble Nebraska origins in order to win the locals' support.

When Rachel Brown reads Hornbeck's column about Cates, she is stunned to hear her outcast friend described as a hero. Public outcry, which Rachel's father stirs up, casts Cates as a villain. The town's conservative politics allows neither for debate nor doubt. Throughout the play, Cates and Drummond encourage Rachel to keep her mind open, while Brown and Brady coax her to abide by their views as they vilify her friend. At the end of the play, Rachel overcomes her fear and recognizes the possibilities of Cates's and Drummond's free thought. She takes her newfound self-reliance with her to the train station, to the city.

MAN VS. SOCIETY

In *Inherit the Wind*, Cates challenges the law and, with it, the norms of Hillsboro society. Facing disfavor from the townspeople, he nonetheless decides to persevere in his cause. Describing his feelings of isolation, Cates explains to Drummond, "People look at me as if I was a murderer. Worse than a murderer!" Drummond, who has learned from his years as a criminal-defense attorney, along with his own struggles as an agnostic and an advocate for unpopular causes, empathizes with Cates. As Drummond says, "It's the loneliest feeling in the world—to find yourself standing up when everybody else is sitting down."

Both Cates and Drummond experience a struggle against mainstream society. The older and more experienced Drummond comforts Cates with his knowledge that individuals make progress for all of society when they courageously pursue the truth regardless of others' opinions. At the end of the play, when the court announces the verdict, Drummond says to Cates, "You don't suppose this kind of thing is ever finished, do you? Tomorrow it'll be something else—and another fella will have to stand up. And you've helped give him the guts to do it!" As Drummond implies, individuals throughout history have challenged societal norms by forcing society to rethink its assumptions. Historical movements appropriate the energy of these individuals to revolutionize society.

Although Brady and Reverend Brown are charismatic public figures, they fail to present themselves as individuals. Rather, they hide behind the Bible and hold themselves up as symbols of society itself. Their efforts to staunch free thought and repress new ideas are anti-individualistic. They maintain order in Hillsboro by scaring people out of having their own opinions and ideas. As the storeowner admits, such individual attitudes are "bad for business." Ultimately, however, Brady's and Brown's fear tactics come up short. Although they technically win the case against Cates, the defense clearly achieves its goal—opening the minds of Hillsboro's townspeople.

MOTIFS

Motifs are recurring structures, contrasts, or literary devices that can help to develop and inform the text's major themes.

LOVE

The romance between Rachel and Cates complicates Rachel's personal development and frames the main conflict of the play—fundamentalism versus freedom of thought—in a personal light. The playwrights portray Reverend Brown, Rachel's father and the community's religious leader, as cruel and heartless. The preacher not only frightens Rachel from a young age but also publicly damns her soul for supporting Cates. Meanwhile, Cates, who teaches evolution to his students and has doubts about religion, stands in bold opposition to Rachel's father and his views. These two characters test Rachel's loyalties throughout the play. Rachel's separation from her father and allegiance with Cates at the end of the trial shows how she resolves this conflict on a personal level, making a story about the politics of ideas a love story as well.

THE CHORUS

The playwrights draw on a traditional dramatic device, the chorus, to underscore the main themes of *Inherit the Wind*. The chorus, which has its origins in ancient Greek theater, is a group of characters who deliver lines—typically sung in verse—that comment on the action of the play and predict the future. In *Inherit the Wind*, the playwrights consolidate this traditional chorus into a single chorus character, the *Baltimore Herald* reporter E. K. Hornbeck. Hornbeck's lines appear in poetic form, and his musings, which originally seem extreme, eventually prove accurate and insightful. His presence also highlights the differences between North and South as well as between urban and rural environments. Hornbeck stands in for the real-life Baltimore journalist H. L. Mencken, one of the most popular journalists in American history, whose coverage of the Scopes Monkey Trial electrified the nation.

SYMBOLS

Symbols are objects, characters, figures, or colors used to represent abstract ideas or concepts.

GOLDEN DANCER

Golden Dancer, a rocking horse Drummond received from his parents as a child, represents the deceptiveness of external beauty. Despite its bright shine and color, the horse broke the first time Drummond rode it. Drummond uses this symbol to convey to Cates the importance of the search for truth and the exposure of people and ideas for what they truly are. As Drummond instructs Cates, "Bert, whenever you see something bright, shining, perfect-seeming—all gold, with purple spots—look behind the paint! And if it's a lie—show it up for what it really is!" Cates, whose classroom microscope reveals physical realities that the naked eye cannot see, is already familiar with this principle. Drummond's words, however, help Cates to realize that his defeat in court may actually be a victory for his cause.

RADIO

When the radio man enters the courtroom to record the trial, the recording marks the first time a trial is broadcast nationally in the United States. In fact, the *Scopes* trial, the inspiration for *Inherit the Wind*, marked that occasion in real life. The radio symbolizes the rapid technological advancement of early twentieth-century America and the consequences of that technology for traditional rural life. The radio also recalls the modern technological devices that Drummond challenges Brady and his witnesses to conceive of in biblical terms—a key element of his argument that ultimately wins over the courtroom audience.

SYMBOLS

SUMMARY & ANALYSIS

ACT ONE, SCENE I

SUMMARY

> HOWARD: *What're yuh skeered of? You was a worm once!*
> MELINDA: *(Shocked) I wasn't neither.*
> HOWARD: *You was so! When the whole world was covered with water, there was nothin' but worms and blobs of jelly. And you and your whole family was worms!*
>
> *(See* QUOTATIONS, *p. 43)*

Outside the courthouse in the small Southern town of Hillsboro, a boy named Howard carries a fishing pole and scours the ground for worms. A girl, Melinda, calls out to him. Howard holds up a worm, and Melinda expresses disgust, but Howard tells her she shouldn't be scared because she herself was once a worm—in fact, her whole family was once worms or blobs of jelly. Melinda threatens to tell her father what Howard has said and warns him that he'll get his mouth washed out with soap. Howard calls Melinda's father a monkey, and Melinda runs away.

Rachel, the Hillsboro minister's daughter, enters. She watches Howard hold up a worm and ask it what it wants to be when it grows up. Mr. Meeker, the bailiff, comes out of the courthouse and greets Rachel. Rachel asks Meeker not to tell her father that she visited the courthouse. She asks to see Bert Cates. Meeker comments that Cates, a schoolteacher, is a more dignified guest than most people usually held in the town jail. Meeker brings Cates up to the courthouse to talk to Rachel.

Cates reminds Rachel that he told her not to visit him. She gives him some clothes from his room at his boarding house. She pleads with him to tell the authorities that his alleged crime—teaching evolution in the local school—was meant as a joke and to promise them he'll never break that law again. Cates changes the subject and speaks about Matthew Harrison Brady, a famous political figure who is due to arrive in Hillsboro to act as a prosecutor in Cates's trial.

Rachel asks Cates why he can't admit he was wrong. Cates says he merely taught his biology class straight from a textbook about Charles Darwin's *On the Origin of Species*. Rachel points out that what Cates did was illegal and that everyone thinks he is wrong. Cates admits that he broke the law but says that his actions are more complicated than simple good and evil. Rachel scolds him for trying to stir things up and asks him why he can't do the right thing. Cates asks whether she means she wants him to do things her father's way. Upset, Rachel runs away. Cates catches up to her and they embrace. When Meeker enters, Rachel breaks the embrace and departs. Meeker marvels at Brady's imminent arrival and asks Cates about his lawyer. Cates explains that a Baltimore newspaper is sending a lawyer to represent him. After joking for a bit, Meeker and Cates exit.

At the general store, the storekeeper opens up for business. He and a woman from town discuss the heat. Rachel's father, the stern Reverend Brown, enters. Two workmen arrive to put up a banner welcoming Brady to town. Reverend Brown says that he wants Brady to know how faithful the community is as soon as he arrives. The workmen start to raise the banner. A local man rushes in and says that Brady's train has arrived. The workmen unfurl the banner, which displays the words "Read Your Bible!" The crowd applauds.

E. K. Hornbeck, a journalist, enters. Townspeople approach him and try to sell him things, but he rebuffs them with sarcastic jokes. Elijah, an illiterate mountain man hawking Bibles, asks Hornbeck whether he is an evolutionist. Hornbeck identifies himself as a journalist from the *Baltimore Herald*. Hornbeck spots an organ-grinder carrying a monkey. In jest, he asks the monkey if it has come to town to act as a witness in the trial. Melinda hands the monkey a penny, and Hornbeck points out that the monkey's greed is the best evidence yet that it is the ancestor of the human race.

A boy appears and announces Brady's arrival. The townspeople sing a hymn and go off to welcome Brady. Hornbeck remains behind with the storekeeper and asks him his opinion on evolution. The storekeeper claims not to have opinions because they could pose a threat to his business. The townspeople cheer and return singing another hymn. They carry pro-Brady and anti-evolutionist banners.

The mayor asks Brady to deliver a speech. The tall, charismatic Brady thanks the townspeople and says he intends to prosecute the arrogant Cates in order to defend Hillsboro from the ideological aggression of Northern cities. The mayor starts to give a speech welcoming Brady, but a photographer and Mrs. Brady interrupt him.

Brady asks the spiritual leader of the community to join them for a photograph, and Reverend Brown steps up. The mayor skips to the end of his speech and declares Brady an honorary colonel in the state militia.

The mayor reports that the local Ladies' Aid club has prepared a brunch for the occasion. As Brady eats, Davenport, the district attorney, introduces himself and says he is eager to work on Brady's team. Mrs. Brady reminds her husband not to overeat. Brady asks about the defendant, Cates. Rachel interjects that she knows Cates and says that he is not a criminal. Brady takes Rachel away from the crowd to talk privately. One man asks the mayor who the defense attorney will be. Hornbeck announces that the *Baltimore Herald* has sent the famous Henry Drummond of Chicago to defend Cates. Reverend Brown reviles Drummond as an agent of the devil.

Brady and Rachel return. Reverend Brown and the mayor try to think of ways to prevent Drummond from entering Hillsboro. Brady insists that instead they should welcome Drummond because the world will pay attention to a victory over someone of Drummond's prominence. Brady explains that he'll easily be able to convict Cates based on what Rachel has told him in private. Brady retires to his suite at the Mansion House. Everyone follows him away except Rachel and Hornbeck, who move to the courthouse.

Rachel calls out for Meeker and then for Cates, asking what she's supposed to do. Hornbeck jokingly offers her his counsel at cut rates. Rachel asks Hornbeck why he is in the courtroom. He shows her a copy of the *Baltimore Herald* in which he wrote an article comparing Cates to Dreyfus, Socrates, and Romeo. Rachel, surprised that Hornbeck has taken Cates's side, expresses frustration that the Hillsboro townspeople would never read articles that portray Cates as a hero.

Hornbeck and Rachel discuss teaching. Rachel says she has no reason to teach material outside the superintendent's guidelines. Hornbeck raises questions about human existence, which Rachel says the Bible answers. Rachel asks how Cates could be innocent if a popular hero like Brady is against him. Hornbeck retorts that Brady ceased to be a spokesman for ordinary Americans when they learned to think for themselves. Rachel and Hornbeck exit.

Back at the storefront, Hornbeck strolls and the storekeeper closes up. The organ-grinder comes onstage with the monkey, and Melinda gives the monkey a penny. Henry Drummond, a thick, slouching man, enters. Seeing Drummond in front of the bright red of the setting sun, Melinda exclaims, "It's the Devil!" Hornbeck greets Drummond, saying "Hello, Devil. Welcome to Hell."

ANALYSIS

The introductory note that precedes Act One establishes that *Inherit the Wind* does not adhere strictly to the factual details of the Scopes Monkey Trial, which frees the playwrights to deliver universally applicable lessons about humankind in the modern age. In twentieth-century America, the advancement of technology and ideas often outpaced the general population's ability to digest and understand them. The reconciliation of science and religion remains an issue to this day, and perspectives restricted by religion, politics, or nationality often impede individual freedom of thought and expression. This tension manifested itself in the debate over evolution in the 1920s, just as the debate over the ethical implications of human cloning stirs similar controversy today.

The playwrights hint at one of *Inherit the Wind*'s major themes—the conflict between urban and rural attitudes—in their description of the setting of the opening scene. They stress that Hillsboro should appear a "sleepy, obscure country town about to be vigorously awakened." The natural state of Hillsboro is static—a condition that is disrupted by the arrival of prominent strangers from cities in the first scene.

The opening lines of the play introduce the central conflict: that of creationism versus evolutionism. As befits a play about the meaning of education, the first characters onstage are children. Howard and Melinda enact the conflict troubling the town in miniature. Howard accuses Melinda's father of being a monkey, while she, in turn, accuses Howard of "sinful talk." Melinda's reaction mirrors the outrage of Hillsboro's authorities and adults about Cates's teaching of evolution theory in public school. Howard, meanwhile, attempts to convey Cates's ideas about evolution but betrays a distorted understanding of these new ideas. Evolution does not equate men with monkeys, but rather posits that the two species share common ancestors. When Howard asks a worm what he wants to be when he grows up, what he really means to ask is what the worm wants its species to become when it evolves. Howard's misunderstanding humorously illustrates the ways in which young minds can internalize and distort new ideas.

The Hillsboro townspeople, aside from Cates, Rachel, and Reverend Brown, form a composite character, and function as a barometer for atmosphere surrounding the trial. Their sense of festivity in welcoming Brady to Hillsboro demonstrates the town's unquestioning embrace of Christian fundamentalism and the significance of this trial in such a quiet, rural town. The playwrights convey the townspeople's lack of sophistication through their dialect and the content of their words. The mountain man Elijah's illiteracy emphasizes Hillsboro's lack of progress. The fact that an illiterate man sells Bibles adds a layer of irony, for Elijah believes in and profits from a book he can't even read himself. Indeed, a significant portion of Hillsboro's townspeople are illiterate, so Reverend Brown's authority as an interpreter of Scripture carries extra weight.

Brady, who arrives in a flurry of gluttony and arrogance, betrays the ignorance and fear at the root of his religious fundamentalism. Although Brady professes his disgust at the idea of evolution, he knows next to nothing about Charles Darwin's work. One of *Inherit the Wind*'s recurring arguments, which Drummond later makes explicit in his defense of Cates, is that it is unjust to reject ideas without examining them. When Brady hears that Drummond will oppose him in the trial, he and the mayor discuss banning Drummond from Hillsboro as a public health hazard. Though absurd, this suggestion is not all that different from the Hillsboro legislature's law against instruction in evolution—both show how figures of authority can use their power to spread fear of the unknown among those they govern.

E. K. Hornbeck provides crucial commentary throughout *Inherit the Wind*. The playwrights use him to transmit their opinions to the audience—a logical choice, for Hornbeck stands in for the real-life journalist and critic H. L. Mencken, whose reporting on the Scopes trial served as a critical source for the playwrights. Hornbeck's quips also provide comic relief in an otherwise weighty work. Although it often appears, especially early in the play, that Hornbeck's comments are addressed to no one but himself, he serves as a chorus character for the playwrights' attitudes toward religion and the events of the trial. Echoing the choruses of ancient Greek drama, Hornbeck's lines appear in verse form, and his predictions, which initially seem extreme, eventually prove true as the play progresses. His presence accentuates the differences between urban and rural attitudes as he editorializes that the rural South lags behind the rest of the nation in coming to terms with the changing times.

ACT ONE, SCENE II

SUMMARY

Several days later, the prosecution (Brady and Davenport) and the defense (Drummond) interview townspeople to serve as members of the jury. The scene opens during of the prosecution's questioning of a local man, Bannister. Davenport asks Bannister whether he attends church. Bannister answers, "Only on Sundays," and Davenport approves him as a juror. Drummond asks Bannister whether he has read about evolution or Darwin, and whether he reads the Bible. Bannister says he is illiterate, and Drummond approves him as a juror.

Before the bailiff calls the next juror, Brady asks the judge if the people in the courtroom may remove their coats because of the heat. The judge agrees. When people remove their coats, Drummond's bright purple suspenders are revealed, prompting hoots from the crowd. Brady asks Drummond if his suspenders reflect the latest fashions in Chicago. To Brady's embarrassment, Drummond replies that he bought the suspenders in Brady's Nebraska hometown.

The judge pounds his gavel and demands order. A man named Dunlap is next to be interviewed. Davenport asks Dunlap whether he believes in the Bible. Dunlap replies that he believes in the word of God and in Brady. The audience cheers Dunlap, and Davenport accepts him as a juror. Drummond, however, refuses Dunlap without questioning him. Brady objects. Drummond replies that he wouldn't object to Brady dismissing an evolutionist as a juror. To go through the formality of questioning Dunlap, Drummond asks him, "How are you?" Dunlap replies "Kinda hot," and Drummond again dismisses him.

Brady objects to Drummond's levity. Although the judge doesn't sustain Brady's objection, he admits to agreeing with him. The judge addresses Brady as "Colonel Brady," which prompts Drummond to object to Brady's title on the grounds that he doesn't know much about Brady's record as a soldier. The judge explains that Brady received the title as an honor. Drummond claims that Brady's title harms Cates's case. The judge gestures to the mayor, who says that he can't take back Brady's honorary title but says he will temporarily grant Drummond the title of colonel as well.

The judge calls the court to order. A man named Sillers is next to be interviewed. Davenport asks Sillers whether he is religious, and Sillers claims to be as religious as anyone else in Hillsboro. Brady steps up and asks Sillers whether he has any children. Sillers replies that he does not. Brady outlines a hypothetical situation in which Sillers's child came home describing a "Godless teacher." Drummond objects, and the judge sustains the objection. Brady asks Sillers whether he has any opinions that might prejudice him in the case. Sillers says he knows Cates only as a customer, not personally. Brady accepts Sillers as a juror.

Drummond asks Sillers whether he puts much effort into religion. Sillers says he focuses on his job while his wife tends to religious matters for both of them. Drummond recasts Sillers's response by suggesting that he takes care of the matters of life on earth while his wife prepares both of them for the afterlife. Davenport objects, and the judge sustains the objection. Drummond asks Sillers whether he has ever encountered a man named Charles Darwin. Sillers says he only lately heard of Darwin. Drummond asks Sillers whether he would have Darwin over for dinner. Brady begins to object, but Drummond cuts him off. Davenport also objects, but Drummond says he is trying to confirm that Sillers puts equally small effort into matters of religion and evolution. Sillers points out that he merely works at the feed store. Drummond approves him as a juror.

Brady starts to retract his approval of Sillers, but Drummond objects. Brady cites a previous case in which he claims that Drummond tricked the jury. Drummond counters that he is attempting to defend the Constitution against those who oppose progress. The judge points out that constitutional matters are decided in a federal court. Drummond says he has to defend the Constitution somewhere.

The judge declares both sides out of order, states that jury selection is complete, and reminds the audience that Reverend Brown is holding a prayer meeting that evening. Drummond objects, claiming that the reminder is unfair. The judge says he is not aware of a meeting of evolutionists. Drummond says that the "Read Your Bible!" banner should be countered with a "Read Your Darwin!" banner. The judge calls the idea preposterous and declares recess. A crowd follows Brady out of the courtroom.

Rachel implores Drummond to call off the trial and asks Cates to beg forgiveness. Drummond asks Cates what he wants to do, and Cates says that the trial resembles a circus. Drummond jokes about the case, and Rachel scolds him for making light of a grave situation. Drummond apologizes to Rachel and describes his respect for Cates. He says he will give up the case only if Cates honestly believes he did wrong. Cates wavers but then firmly states that he will continue to stand trial. Rachel protests, but Cates asks her to support him. Upset, Rachel admits that Brady may call her to testify against Cates. Cates is shocked. As Meeker leads him back to his cell, Cates cries out that the jury will "crucify" him if Rachel reveals the content of their private conversations.

Drummond and Rachel talk. Rachel says that Brady scares her less than her father, Reverend Brown. She recalls being frightened as a child because she never knew her mother and greatly feared her father. Rachel asks Drummond if Cates is evil. Drummond calls Cates a good man and encourages Rachel to lend Cates her support.

> The man who has everything figured out is probably a fool. College examinations notwithstanding, it takes a very smart fella to say "I don't know the answer!"
> (See QUOTATIONS, p. 43)

ANALYSIS

As in the first scene, the playwrights communicate some of the key thematic ideas of *Inherit the Wind* in its stage directions. As the scene opens on the courtroom, "[t]he shapes of the buildings are dimly visible in the background, as if Hillsboro itself were on trial." Indeed, the drama of the courtroom scenes plays out against the ever-present backdrop of the town and its people. This rural, conservative, and religious Southern town opposes the members of the defense, who must struggle to gain a voice for their ideas—concepts that much of contemporary society accepts as elementary biology.

The three potential jurors in this scene are similar, typical townspeople of Hillsboro. None of them betrays strong convictions or exceptional intelligence. Although all of them profess to be Christians, none stand out on the basis of extraordinary faith. Bannister emphasizes his eagerness to watch the trial from the jury box, like a show. His illiteracy, like that of the mountain man Elijah, points to Hillsboro's backwardness. Dunlap differentiates himself by professing membership in the Matthew Harrison Brady cult of personality, and Drummond rejects him on these grounds. Drummond's interrogation of Sillers is the first sign that the religious faith of the Hillsboro townspeople may not run much deeper than simple conformity. When Sillers admits that he leaves religion to his wife, we see the townspeople's Christianity in a new light. We know that people in Hillsboro go to church and profess a belief in God, but we now wonder whether such behavior may be mere formality paid as a price of citizenship in the town, a lip service empty of spiritual meaning. Drummond exposes Sillers's flimsy religious faith by probing deeper than Brady or the other people of Hillsboro are capable. Sillers may not be an atheist or an agnostic like Drummond, but his convictions do not run deep.

This first courtroom scene highlights important differences between Brady and Drummond—in background, perspective, manners, and behavior—that recur in their interactions throughout the play. They serve as foils to each other, as each accentuates the distinct traits of the other. While *Inherit the Wind* as a whole explores an abstract conflict between religious fundamentalism and freedom of thought, the face-to-face conflict between the forceful personalities of Brady and Drummond lends this conflict a physical embodiment. Because the trial, in part, depends on the mood of the town and the opinions of its residents, each attorney attempts to win the audience's respect, recognizing that the crowd will influence the judge and jury.

Brady tries to alienate Drummond from the courtroom crowd by harping on Drummond's suspenders, attempting to cast him as a freak from the big city. But Drummond's fashion choice proves to be premeditated, for he turns the tables on Brady by telling the crowd he bought the suspenders in Brady's Nebraska hometown. This unexpected twist marks Brady's first moment of embarrassment before a crowd that is predisposed to support him. Drummond continues to use this strategy—turning Brady's own words and attitudes against him—to humorous and ironic effect throughout the trial.

Brady enters the trial with a distinct advantage. Reputed for his fundamentalist Christian principles, he receives a warm welcome from the townspeople and an honorary title from the mayor. Although Drummond argues that this title lends the prosecution an unfair symbolic advantage, his objection is laced with irony and humor. Whereas Brady clearly enjoys the meaningless distinction and celebrates it with a swollen sense of self-importance, Drummond chuckles when the judge reluctantly grants him a similar title. To Drummond, titles hold little significance in comparison to the reality of action and deed. Brady, however, leans on these titles for a sense of moral authority. Drummond's ironic appropriation of Brady's title is the second step in his humiliation of his opponent.

Drummond opposes the "commercial announcement" of the prayer meeting and the public signs commanding people to read their Bibles. Although this approach initially strikes the judge and the townspeople as preposterous, Drummond's complaints ultimately make the townspeople reconsider the differences between secular Darwinism and officially endorsed Christianity. Although Drummond does not mention it explicitly, he points to one of the founding principles of American democracy—the separation of church and state. By demanding fair treatment for evolution theory under the law, Drummond plants in his listeners' minds the idea that Christian authorities may not have a monopoly on the truth. He reemphasizes this point later in the trial by demonstrating the Bible's inability to explain modern machinery.

After casting Drummond as the devil incarnate, Brady leaves the courtroom with tremendous public support. Brady departs like a "shepherd leading his flock" while Drummond leaves alone. But Drummond's solitude does not faze him. Although he is vilified before the public, he remains confident in his convictions because he values his own search for truth over the opinions of the crowd. In contrast, Brady's reliance on public support foreshadows his later collapse after his humiliation before the courtroom audience.

The scene closes with Rachel's description of her relationship with her father, which provides insight into her fear for Cates and her efforts to convince him to confess his guilt. Rachel's fear of her father originated in her early childhood and still runs deep. Given Reverend Brown's position of authority in the community, Rachel has never been able to overcome her fear. Caught between the bond of family that dictates loyalty to her father and the budding love that pulls her toward Cates and his cause, Rachel suffers from fear and confusion. Her confession of fear of her father foreshadows his public disowning and damning of her in the next scene.

ACT TWO, SCENE I

SUMMARY

On the courthouse lawn, two workmen discuss what to do about the "Read Your Bible!" banner. One of them says they should leave it up. Brady walks up, followed by a crowd of reporters, all of them except Hornbeck taking notes. A British reporter asks Brady his opinion of Drummond. Brady admits that the two of them were once friends and that Drummond supported his 1908 presidential campaign. He counters that even if is own brother, much less Drummond, were challenging popular belief in the Bible, that would not stop him from standing up for his beliefs.

Brady dismisses the reporters and then strikes up conversation with Hornbeck. Brady calls Hornbeck's reporting biased, and Hornbeck responds that he writes as a critic, not an objective reporter. Brady invites Hornbeck to Reverend Brown's prayer meeting, and Hornbeck says he won't miss it. Hornbeck walks off, and Reverend Brown, escorting Mrs. Brady, approaches Brady. After some chit-chat, Reverend Brown strikes up the prayer meeting sternly from the podium. Drummond enters and receives glares from the preacher. To quick response from the crowd, Reverend Brown runs through the story of God's creation of the world as told in the Book of Genesis. Rachel enters in the midst of the crescendo of call and response.

As Reverend Brown's back-and-forth oration with the crowd reaches a frenzied pitch, the preacher asks the crowd if they curse and cast out the man who denies the story of Genesis, referring to Cates by pointing at the jail. The crowd responds furiously, which causes Rachel to shake. Reverend Brown asks the crowd if they should pray for God to bring his hellfire down on Cates. He goes further, comparing Cates to the Pharaohs and asking for "his soul [to] writhe in anguish and damnation." Rachel interrupts and asks her father to stop condemning Cates. Reverend Brown calls out for the Lord to punish those who want to forgive Cates.

Brady, who has been growing uncomfortable with Reverend Brown's sermon, interrupts. He cautions Reverend Brown and suggests that the preacher should not try to "destroy that which you hope to save." Brady quotes the book of Proverbs and reminds the crowd of the Christian message of forgiveness before dismissing them. The crowd leaves, singing "Go, Tell It On the Mountain."

After the crowd is gone, Brady approaches Drummond. Reminding Drummond of their former friendship, Brady asks why Drummond has abandoned him. Drummond replies, "All motion is relative. Perhaps it is you who have moved away—by standing still." These words surprise Brady, and after a moment of startled silence, he walks backward offstage, leaving Drummond alone.

ANALYSIS

The fundamentalist and evolutionist factions in the play come into starker conflict in this scene. Whereas Drummond's compassion for Rachel at the end of Act I delineates kindness as the mark of an open mind, the events of the prayer meeting thrust us back to the fundamentalist perspective. By constantly shifting between these perspectives, *Inherit the Wind* works as dramatic theater, presenting one confrontation after another.

When the workmen who appear at the beginning of the scene decide to leave the "Read Your Bible!" sign in its place, one workman declares, "The Devil don't run this town. Leave it up," echoing Hornbeck's ironic greeting of Drummond at the end of the first scene. The playwrights juxtapose Drummond's compassion and understanding for Cates and Rachel at the end of Act I with the workmen's knee-jerk vilification of Drummond as the devil.

As Reverend Brown approaches the platform to deliver his sermon, the stage directions emphasize Hillsboro's enthusiastic reception of its spiritual leader: "The prayer meeting is motion picture, radio, and tent-show to these people. To them, the Reverend Brown is a combination Milton Sills and Douglas Fairbanks." In this rural community, religion is not only a guide for moral conduct but also a primary source of entertainment. The playwrights' comparison of Reverend Brown to Milton Sills and Douglas Fairbanks—popular film stars during the era of the Scopes trial—emphasizes this point. Likewise, the style in which Reverend Brown delivers his sermons resembles theater more than teaching. At the end of the scene, we are left with the sense that fundamentalist Christianity monopolizes the townspeople's worldview. We feel that the residents of Hillsboro may only profess their faith in this brand of Christianity because small-town life has exposed them to little else. More exposure to science, literature, or philosophy might cause them to waver in their beliefs or to investigate and define them more critically. Indeed, the townspeople's shifting allegiances near the end of the play confirm these possibilities.

The extreme nature of Brown's sermon—which damns Cates and all those who support him, including his own daughter—leads Brady to voice a different opinion, one that contradicts Hillsboro's brand of fundamentalism. With Brown having whipped the crowd into a zealous frenzy, Brady becomes uncomfortable and outright objects to Brown's treatment of his daughter. Brady reminds Brown of a quote from the Bible, "He that troubleth his own house . . . shall inherit the wind." Brady implies that Brown, by bringing condemnation on his own daughter, will leave himself with nothing but his own hot air. In this departure, Brady distinguishes himself from Brown and his docile Hillsboro followers by advocating the Christian practice of forgiveness. When Brown curses his own daughter, practically with glee, Brady reminds him that his mission is to save human souls—not to hasten their damnation. Unlike Brown's fire-and-brimstone sermonizing, which draws heavily from parts of the Old Testament, Brady emphasizes the more forgiving New Testament doctrines of Jesus. Although Brady does display his share of weaknesses, notably his vanity and ceremonious self-importance, his reaction to Brown's sermon implies that he possesses a compassionate streak that Brown lacks.

Act Two, Scene II

Summary

> *The individual human mind. In a child's power to master the multiplication table there is more sanctity than in all your shouted "Amens!", "Holy, Holies!" and "Hosannahs!" An idea is a greater monument than a cathedral. And the advance of man's knowledge is more of a miracle than any sticks turned to snakes, or the parting of waters!*
>
> *(See* Quotations, *p. 44)*

Two days later, the trial is in full swing. The scene opens with the young Howard on the witness stand. Howard explains to Brady the scientific theory that Cates taught him in school. Howard says, "Man was sort of evoluted. From the 'Old World Monkeys.'" Brady mocks this theory and asks whether Cates ever mentioned God in his teachings. Howard says no. Brady begins what seems like a speech, but Drummond objects. Brady claims that he wasn't about to make a speech but then derides evolutionists at length. The crowd applauds.

Drummond asks Howard what he thinks of Darwin and the theory Cates taught him. Davenport objects, but Drummond says he is trying to establish that Howard has the right to think. The judge and Brady insist that establishing the right to think is not the mission of the trial at hand. Drummond rephrases his question to ask Howard whether the theory of evolution has harmed him in any way. Brady objects, and the judge sustains the objection.

Drummond asks Howard if he believes the theory Cates taught him. Howard says he isn't sure and has to think about it. Drummond asks Howard whether he thinks modern technologies like tractors and telephones are evil because the Bible doesn't mention them. Brady protests that Drummond is confusing the witness. He asks Drummond whether "right" has any meaning to him. Drummond delivers a speech, claiming that right is meaningless but that truth is valuable "as a direction." He says that a morality of simple right and wrong is arbitrary. Drummond asks Howard whether he understands their discussion. Howard says no, and Drummond dismisses him.

Davenport calls Rachel to the stand. Brady asks her about her acquaintance with Cates and about Cates's religious affiliations. She explains that Cates stopped attending church after a local boy, Tommy Stebbins, drowned in the river while out for a swim. At the funeral, Reverend Brown declared that Tommy wouldn't be saved because he had never been baptized. Cates interjects that Reverend Brown said the boy's soul would burn forever. Dunlap shouts from the audience and calls Cates a sinner. The judge pounds his gavel and demands order. Cates continues to shout that religion should help people rather than cause them fear. The judge again calls for order. Drummond requests that Cates's statements be stricken from the record, and the judge grants the request.

Brady resumes questioning Rachel about Cates's religious views. Drummond objects on the grounds that hearsay isn't admissible evidence, but the judge lets the question stand. Referring to their private conversation on the day of Brady's arrival, Brady asks Rachel to repeat conversations she had with Cates about religious matters. Rachel falters. Brady quotes Cates as saying that man created God and that human marriage was comparable to the breeding of animals. Drummond objects. Rachel, visibly upset, claims that Brady is misquoting a joke Cates made. She goes silent, and Brady dismisses her. At Cates's request, Drummond also dismisses Rachel.

Davenport states that the prosecution has no further witnesses. Drummond then attempts to call to the stand three scientists. Brady objects to the testimony of experts on evolution, and the judge sustains the objection. Drummond argues that testimony of scientists in this case is no different from testimony of forensics experts in a murder case. Drummond then asks the judge whether he would admit testimony on the Bible. When the judge agrees to allow such testimony, Drummond calls Brady to the stand. Davenport objects. The judge calls Drummond's request strange, but Brady agrees to take the stand.

Drummond asks Brady about his familiarity with the Bible and with Darwin's work. Brady says that he knows much of the Bible by memory but that he has never read Darwin. Drummond asks Brady how he can reject a book he has never read. Davenport objects. The judge orders Drummond to confine his questions to matters regarding the Bible. Drummond asks Brady whether he believes that every word in the Bible should be taken literally. Brady says that he does. Drummond then asks Brady about the episode of Jonah and the whale, and Brady says he believes that God is capable of miracles. Drummond asks about the story of Joshua causing the sun to stop, and Brady again affirms his belief in God's power to perform miracles. Drummond asks Brady if he is aware of the implications of the sun stopping in the sky according to the modern theory of the solar system. Drummond asks Brady if he denies the teachings of Copernicus as well as Darwin. Brady replies that God's will supercedes natural laws. Drummond asks several more questions relating to the Bible, and Davenport interrupts to raise doubts about the relevance of Drummond's line of questioning. Brady says Drummond is playing into the prosecution's hands by demonstrating the defense's contempt for sacred things.

Drummond says that progress has a price and that the new understandings Darwin has brought to us demand that we surrender our faith in the literal truth of the Bible. Brady protests. Drummond asks Brady why God gave man the power to think if he didn't intend for him to use it. Drummond asks Brady the difference between a man and a sponge. Brady, faltering, says that God's will determines the difference between a man and a sponge. Dramatically, Drummond declares that Cates merely wants the same God-given right as a sponge—the right to think. The crowd, for the first time, applauds Drummond.

Brady calls Cates deluded. Drummond says that Cates merely lacks Brady's clear-cut notions of right and wrong. Drummond calmly walks up to one of the scientists he intended to call to the witness stand and takes from him a small rock. Drummond asks Brady how old he figures the rock is. Brady says he isn't interested in the rock's age. Drummond cites one scholar's claim that the rock is ten million years old. Brady claims that the rock can't be more than six thousand years old because one biblical scholar determined 4004 B.C. to be the year of creation. Drummond asks Brady whether creation happened during a twenty-four-hour day and whether that day can be considered a day at all, given that the creation of the world preceded the creation of the sun. Drummond suggests that Brady's supposed first "day" may in fact have been ten million years in duration.

The crowd becomes excited, and the judge calls for order. Brady accuses Drummond of attempting to destroy the people's faith in the Bible. Drummond says that the Bible is a good book but that it isn't the sole source of human knowledge. Brady claims that God spoke directly to the Bible's authors. Drummond responds by asking why we shouldn't think that God spoke to Darwin as well. Brady insists that God couldn't have spoken to Darwin because God told Brady so. To the crowd's amusement, Drummond mocks Brady's claim to be the mouthpiece of God. Exasperated, Brady backs down momentarily and claims that every man has free will. Drummond asks why, if every man has free will, Cates is in jail. Brady begins raving, quoting the Bible, while Drummond continues to mock him, prompting laughter from the crowd.

Drummond dismisses Brady as a witness, but Brady continues to rant. The judge tells Brady to step down and adjourns the trial until the next day. Davenport asks the judge to strike Brady's testimony from the record. Still babbling biblical names, Brady collapses in his chair. As the crowd leaves the courtroom, Mrs. Brady comforts her humiliated husband.

ANALYSIS

The centerpiece of the play, the trial scene careens on the wave of the courtroom crowd's approval, moving from certain triumph for the prosecution to moral victory for the defense. Drummond's ironic, probing questioning of witnesses and Rachel Brown's emotional breakdown at Brady's hands win Cates the crowd's sympathies, and the trial culminates in Drummond's humiliation of the dumbfounded Brady. Once the townspeople clearly demonstrate their support for Cates, the subsequent legal consequences he faces take on secondary importance.

The questioning of Howard, more so than that of any other witness, brings the specific conflict of the trial—creationism versus evolutionism—to an abstract level. Drummond argues to the court, "I am trying to establish, Your Honor, that Howard—or Colonel Brady—or Charles Darwin—or anyone in the courtroom—or you, sir—has the right to think!" When the judge responds that "the right to think is not on trial here," Drummond barks back that the right to think "is very much on trial," that it "is fearfully in danger in the proceedings of this court!" But regardless of the validity of Drummond's argument, the nature of the American legal system limits it. Cates is on trial in a local court for breaking a law. Drummond, in his argument, does not challenge Cates's guilt or innocence so much as the justice of the law itself, with respect to the Constitution of the United States. As we see at the end of the play, to make this challenge real, Drummond must bring it to a higher court.

The playwrights continually demonstrate their support for the evolutionists' side by contrasting the defense's compassion with the fundamentalists' callous superiority. When Rachel takes the witness stand, Brady asks her to recount Cates's reasons for his separation from the church community. Rachel recalls her father's declaration that young Tommy Stebbins, who drowned to death, would be eternally damned because he was never baptized. Through the description of this event and of Cates's departure from Hillsboro's religious community, the playwrights illustrate Cates's own moral development independent from organized religion. Cates declares to the court, "Religion's supposed to comfort people, isn't it? Not frighten them to death!" In this sympathetic portrayal, Cates emerges not as an atheist or an agnostic but as an individual who could not, in good conscience, abide by the cruel morality of the church.

Drummond's argument emphasizes the distinction between "truth," which he believes every man has a right to seek for himself, and absolute values of right and wrong as determined by religious authorities. Drummond implies that individuals and groups who use faith to stake their claims to righteousness often employ religion as a vehicle or justification for immoral pursuits. Reverend Brown, in his monomaniacal campaign to instill fear in the hearts of the people of Hillsboro, uses religion to buttress his authority. Although Brown enjoys respect from the townspeople, his condemnations of his own daughter and of Tommy Stebbins reveal his heartless interior. Cates, meanwhile, although he has broken the law and expressed doubts about religion, comes across as a compassionate figure. He stands up for Rachel and sincerely mourns Tommy Stebbins as a young life cut off too soon. Despite his status as a legal and religious outsider, Cates embodies a kindness and compassion that stand in sharp contrast to Reverend Brown's unforgiving scorn.

Drummond suffers several procedural setbacks during the trial but makes his argument nonetheless. He uses Howard's testimony to demonstrate that evolution represents human possibility rather than denial of God. Next, Drummond equates evolution with modern innovations, like the tractor, that have become essential elements in rural life. When the judge denies the scientific experts the opportunity to testify, Drummond uses Brady to show that a literal interpretation of the Bible leads into a web of contradictions. Although these tactics fail to exonerate Cates, they go a long way in discrediting his persecutors.

During the course of the questioning, the playwrights juxtapose the personalities and philosophies of Brady and Drummond. The stage directions differentiate the opponents: "The courtroom seems to resent Drummond's gentle ridicule of the orator. To many, there is an effrontery in Drummond's very voice—folksy and relaxed. It's rather like a harmonica following a symphony concert." Drummond's delivery involves little ornamentation or finesse. Brady, on the other hand, uses a lengthy and grandiose style of oration that initially appeals to the court. But when the substance of Brady's argument contradicts itself and his hubris becomes clear, Brady loses his popularity and support, while Drummond's perseverance, grit, logic, and playful irony win over the courtroom.

ACT THREE

SUMMARY

> *All shine, and no substance!*
>
> *(See* QUOTATIONS, *p. 44)*

The next day, the courtroom audience awaits the jury's verdict. Hornbeck enters and mockingly bows before Brady. Cates and Drummond discuss whether Cates will go to jail. Drummond tells the story of Golden Dancer, a rocking horse he received as a birthday present at age seven. The horse looked beautiful in the store window but broke the first time Drummond tried to ride it.

A radio reporter sets up a microphone. The mayor tells the judge that state authorities are worried about the press coverage surrounding the case. The mayor cautions the judge to "go easy" on Cates should the jury hand down a guilty verdict. The radio reporter warns Drummond not to swear or say the word "God" during the broadcast. The jury returns, and the judge asks for the verdict. Sillers hands the verdict to the judge, who pronounces Cates guilty. The crowd's reaction is loud but mixed.

The judge calls for order and starts to announce a sentence, but Drummond cuts him off, citing the defendant's right to make a statement before sentencing. Cates admits to a lack of public speaking skills and says that he is only a teacher. He calls the law he broke unjust and vows to continue to oppose it. He trails off mid-sentence and sits down.

Glancing at the mayor, the judge declares Cates's punishment to be a $100 fine. Brady angrily demands a harsher sentence. The judge grants Drummond the right to appeal the case to a higher court. Brady asks permission to read a statement, but Drummond objects. The judge instructs Brady to read his remarks to the crowd before declaring the court adjourned.

The courtroom becomes chaotic with screaming children and food vendors. The judge tries several times to get the crowd's attention for Brady's remarks. Finally, Brady begins his triumphant speech, but the radio reporter interrupts and asks him to speak more clearly. When Brady resumes his speech, people start to leave the courtroom. The radio reporter cuts Brady off, saying that a producer in Chicago has told him that their time is up. Brady picks up his speech again after the microphone is removed, but he suddenly freezes up and collapses. Onlookers come to his aid. While Brady is being carried out of the courtroom, he deliriously recites what sounds like an victory speech for a presidential election. Hornbeck makes a half-mocking, half-sympathetic speech about political losers like Brady.

Cates asks Drummond whether he won or lost. Drummond tells Cates he won a moral victory by bringing national attention to his case. Cates submits himself to Meeker to be returned to jail, but Meeker says that Hornbeck and the *Baltimore Herald* have put up $500 for Cates's bail.

Rachel comes in with a suitcase and says she is leaving her father. She hands Cates a book of his and tells him that she read it but didn't understand it. Rachel apologizes to Drummond and says that she always used to be scared of thinking. She concludes that the possibility of thoughts being bad shouldn't prevent people from thinking them.

Suddenly, the judge enters and announces that Brady has died of a "busted belly." Drummond reacts with sadness, but Hornbeck unleashes a sarcastic tirade against Brady, calling him a "Barnum-bunkum Bible-beating bastard." Drummond scolds Hornbeck for deriding Brady's religion, and the two argue about Brady's merits. Drummond calls Brady great, while Hornbeck accuses Drummond of undue sentimentality and predicts that Brady will be forgotten. Hornbeck leaves.

Cates asks Drummond how much an appeal will cost, but Drummond dismisses the issue of cost. In their rush to leave for the train, Rachel and Cates leave behind Cates's copy of Darwin—the book she returned to him. Drummond picks up the copy of Darwin and also picks up the court's copy of the Bible. He holds one in each hand and pretends to balance them like a scale. He then puts both books in his briefcase and walks out of the courtroom and away across the square.

> *You see, I haven't really thought very much. I was always afraid of what I might think — so it seemed safer not to think at all. But now I know. A thought is like a child inside our body. It has to be born. If it dies inside you, part of you dies too!*
>
> *(See* QUOTATIONS, *p. 45)*

ANALYSIS

Early in the play's final scene, as Cates and Drummond discuss the trial, Drummond recounts his childhood love for a rocking horse called "Golden Dancer." Drummond uses the story to warn Cates that shiny appearances may obscure hidden problems and truths. He advises Cates to seek out and expose the truth in any way he can, as a service both to himself and to the public. This lesson relates to Drummond's own personal and professional experiences in searching for the truth as a lawyer. The story also sheds light on Drummond's understated, self-reliant style in the courtroom. Brady, meanwhile, uses an elaborate and showy style of oration that Drummond likens to the rocking horse—it has an appealing exterior but little substance. To Drummond, anyone in search of truth can see beyond Brady's flashy but insubstantial words.

Rachel's development, which is constant throughout the play, becomes complete in the last scene. Although many townspeople open their minds to new ideas during the trial, the playwrights allow us an especially intimate look at Rachel's psychological development. In Rachel, we see the process by which an individual sheds values that have been forced upon her and begins to rely on her own intellect. Of all the characters, Rachel undergoes the most profound personal transformation over the course of the play, ultimately opening her heart to Cates and her mind to new ideas. Her father's status as the religious leader of Hillsboro and her conflicting love for the outcast Cates place Rachel in a painful position. These opposing forces in her life provide an opportunity for growth. At the beginning of the trial, Rachel, longing for a return to "normalcy," urges Cates to admit his guilt. After the trial, however, Rachel abandons her father. This decision demonstrates her full maturity into womanhood, her breaking free from a painful part of her life, and her newfound identification with Cates's cause—freedom of thought and action.

The last few moments of the play, in which Drummond weighs the Bible in one hand against *On the Origin of Species* in the other, carry symbolic significance. During the trial, Drummond has fought for the individual's right to think outside the boundaries prescribed by organized religion. An agnostic, uncertain about the nature and existence of God, Drummond does not demonstrate a strong allegiance to religion. On the other hand, however, he does not seem to embrace evolution wholeheartedly either. Drummond advocates for the individual's right to make up his own mind—or for the right to postpone that choosing. He balances the two books in his hands, as if on scales. This act, which alludes to the scales of justice, represents Drummond's belief that each book has equal worth. As he "half-smiles, half-shrugs" upon exiting the courtroom, he contemplates whether his efforts in Cates's trial have furthered justice.

Important Quotations Explained

1. HOWARD: What're yuh skeered of? You was a worm once!
    MELINDA: (Shocked) I wasn't neither.
    HOWARD: You was so! When the whole world was covered with water, there was nothin' but worms and blobs of jelly. And you and your whole family was worms!

A play intimately concerned with the nature of education, *Inherit the Wind* begins with an appropriate image of two young, inarticulate children discussing a controversial modern theory. Their argument is a miniature form of the play's central conflicts: creationism versus evolutionism and religious orthodoxy versus freedom of thought. Melinda reacts to Howard in the same way that most of the people of Hillsboro react to Bert Cates—she becomes frightened and calls him sinful. Although Howard's grip on evolutionary theory is rudimentary at best, the new ideas to which Cates has exposed him clearly excite Howard. Howard's pronouncements humorously equate humans—specifically Melinda and her family—with monkeys and worms. His disrespect for Melinda's father points to the threat these ideas pose to the social order of a town like Hillsboro.

2. The man who has everything figured out is probably a fool. College examinations notwithstanding, it takes a very smart fella to say "I don't know the answer!"

At the close of Act One, Drummond reassures Rachel that she need not worry about Bert's confused state. These lines emphasize Drummond's belief that intellectual curiosity—which inherently involves uncertainty—is essential to an individual's growth. To Drummond, absolute values close people's minds to the truth, for they restrict people's investigation of problems that might call such values into question. Drummond feels that the human mind demands that any given issue be approached from all possible angles. He rejects a literal interpretation of the Bible as a solution that is reached too easily. Through his questions to Brady, Drummond later proves that such an incessantly literal interpretation of the Bible necessarily contradicts itself. Drummond resists the church because it rigidly dictates the moral behavior of small-town America and forces its members to accept its terms without question. Drummond's ideas, on the other hand, proceed not from answers but from unknowns.

3. The individual human mind. In a child's power to master the multiplication table there is more sanctity than in all your shouted "Amens!", "Holy, Holies!" and "Hosannahs!" An idea is a greater monument than a cathedral. And the advance of man's knowledge is more of a miracle than any sticks turned to snakes, or the parting of waters!

In Act Two, Scene II, Drummond strives to demonstrate to the court the power of the human mind. To Drummond, human intellect has the power to advance humankind, while religion stifles human inquiries. This quotation not only defines one of Drummond's most strongly held personal philosophies but also speaks to the main conflict of the play—that of creationism versus evolutionism—on an abstract level. The Hillsboro townspeople initially see Drummond's words as extreme, for, in their conservative mindset, they see any free thought that questions the Bible as dangerous and blasphemous. However, Drummond's case gains momentum as the trial progresses. He wins over the townspeople by probing witnesses playfully and ironically, exposing the contradictions beneath their too easily assumed beliefs. Ultimately, by trapping Brady in the inconsistencies that riddle his fundamentalist thinking, Drummond turns the tables and changes the momentum of the case.

4. All shine, and no substance! [Turning to Cates] Bert, whenever you see something bright, shining, perfect-seeming—all gold, with purple spots—look behind the paint! And if it's a lie—show it up for what it really is!

At the beginning of Act Three, Drummond, awaiting the court's verdict, speaks to Cates about the importance of an individual's personal search for truth. Drummond recounts the story of the "Golden Dancer," a rocking horse he had been given as a child, to emphasize the importance of this search. Golden Dancer seemed beautiful in the store window but broke into pieces as soon as Drummond rode it, for its manufacturing was shoddy. Drummond uses the story to emphasize the deceptive nature of superficial beauty, as a way to encourage Cates to persevere in searching for the underlying truths of the world for both himself and his community.

5. You see, I haven't really thought very much. I was always afraid of what I might think—so it seemed safer not to think at all. But now I know. A thought is like a child inside our body. It has to be born. If it dies inside you, part of you dies too!

At the end of Act Three, while conversing with Cates and Drummond, Rachel expresses her newfound appreciation for freedom of thought. In doing so, she addresses one of the most important lessons of *Inherit the Wind*. In the playwrights' view, ignorance and fear combine to create conservative, fundamentalist value systems, like the one we see in the Hillsboro townspeople's initial attitudes toward evolution. People cannot accept new ideas if they are not exposed to new ideas. Authority figures like Brady and Reverend Brown repress new, unorthodox thinking out of fear that unconventional ideas might disrupt the social order that they command. Over the course of the trial, Rachel overcomes this ignorance and fear of individual thought and combines this transformation with romantic feelings for Cates. This change in Rachel demonstrates the power of thought and of love.

QUOTATIONS

Key Facts

FULL TITLE
Inherit the Wind

PLAYWRIGHTS
Jerome Lawrence and Robert E. Lee

TYPE OF WORK
Play

GENRE
Courtroom drama

LANGUAGE
English

TIME AND PLACE WRITTEN
Early 1950s; United States

DATE OF FIRST PUBLICATION
1955

PUBLISHER
Random House

TONE
Playful and ironic at times, but often carries weighty symbolic significance

SETTING (TIME)
The playwrights define the setting as "not too long ago," also noting in their notes preceding the play that "It might have been yesterday. It could be tomorrow."

SETTING (PLACE)
A fictional town called Hillsboro, in the rural South; the playwrights imply that these events could have taken place in any small town in America.

PROTAGONIST
Bertram Cates

MAJOR CONFLICT
> After being arrested for teaching evolution to his science classes, Bertram Cates becomes the center of a controversial trial about religious fundamentalism versus the freedom of individual thought.

RISING ACTION
> Cates teaches evolution to his science classes; Cates is arrested for violating the law that bars the teaching of evolution; Matthew Harrison Brady and Henry Drummond represent, respectively, the prosecution and the defense, drawing national attention to the trial.

CLIMAX
> When Brady flounders under Drummond's line of questioning, the courtroom spectators shift their support to Cates.

FALLING ACTION
> Cates and Drummond consider their trial a popular and societal victory and decide to prepare an appeal; Brady becomes flustered and humiliated and, shortly after, dies of a "busted belly"; Rachel leaves her father and learns the power of individual thought.

THEMES
> Fundamentalism vs. freedom of thought; the individual vs. society; the conflict of urban and rural attitudes

MOTIFS
> Love; the chorus

SYMBOLS
> Golden Dancer; Hillsboro

FORESHADOWING
> Brady's gluttonous behavior foreshadows his later death from a "busted belly"; the playwrights' stage directions describe Hillsboro as a "sleepy, obscure country town about to be vigorously awakened," foreshadowing the significance of the trial.

KEY FACTS

STUDY QUESTIONS & ESSAY TOPICS

STUDY QUESTIONS

1. *How does Brady's character relate to the idea of hubris, or pride? How is his character tragic?*

At the beginning of the play, Brady has confidence in his abilities to win the trial. Scornful of the threat that Drummond might present to him as the opposing attorney, Brady never considers the prospect of his subsequent failure. Brady derives his authority from his upholding of the Bible and derives his self-worth from the crowd's reverence of him. The townspeople's initial awe infuses Brady with hubris, with an inflated sense of his own abilities. Later, when he loses their support, his composure crumbles along with his confidence.

Brady ran for president in three consecutive elections but never won. This failure plagues him throughout his life and manifests itself during the trial. When he falls ill following his ranting responses to Drummond's line of questioning, he deliriously spews forth a speech he had prepared for his never-realized presidential victory. When Drummond humiliates Brady with questions that expose the contradictions behind his rigid, literal belief in the Bible, Brady becomes a fallen hero. His death confirms his underwhelming victory in the trial as a profound, fatal disappointment.

2. *What is the significance of the playwrights' description of the setting of the play? What does it say about their attitudes toward Southern fundamentalism?*

Lawrence and Lee mean for us to consider Hillsboro not as an individual town but as a symbol of small towns across America, a symbol of the narrow-mindedness that they believe such towns breed. Distinctions between urban and small-town life recur throughout the play. Urban living inherently exposes people to more diversity than small-town living—and indeed, progressives more often inhabit cities than they do small towns. In cities, rapid urbanization, immigration, and technological improvements expose city dwellers to a wide range of new ideas.

In *Inherit the Wind*, the playwrights relate the struggle of fundamentalism against progressivism to the struggle of conservative farmers against the policies of more liberal city-dwellers. The playwrights place the townspeople of Hillsboro, with their rural dialect, dress, and behavior—some of them illiterate—in contrast with E. K. Hornbeck and Henry Drummond, sophisticated and eloquent city dwellers. Reverend Brown, the most visible figure of authority in Hillsboro, displays an extreme narrow-mindedness that has no room for the compassion we see in the urban, agnostic Drummond.

3. *What purpose does Cates and Rachel's romantic relationship serve in* INHERIT THE WIND*?*

Rachel's relationship with Cates speeds her personal development and highlights the main conflict of the play—fundamentalism versus freedom of thought—in a personal and dramatic way. Throughout the play, Rachel is caught in a bind between her father, Reverend Brown, and her romantic interest, Cates. The cruel and heartless Reverend Brown not only has frightened Rachel from a young age but also rants at a town prayer meeting that her soul is damned for supporting Cates. Cates, meanwhile, as a liberal teacher who has conveyed the theory of evolution to his students, stands in bold opposition to Rachel's father and his views. These two characters test Rachel's loyalties until Rachel ultimately decides to leave her father and side with Cates at the conclusion of the trial. In this choice, Rachel demonstrates her recognition of the value of free thought and her rejection of the confining, fundamentalist thinking of her father's church community.

Suggested Essay Topics

1. *What is the fundamental conflict in* INHERIT THE WIND? *Discuss the ways in which the playwrights support this theme through their characters and motifs.*

2. *Why do the playwrights imply, in their note preceding the play, that the themes of their play are timeless and universal? What relevance do these themes have today?*

3. *How does Melinda and Howard's interaction in the first scene of* INHERIT THE WIND *foreshadow the play's main theme?*

4. *Discuss the historical context of* INHERIT THE WIND *in terms of the Scopes trial and the rapidly changing society of the United States in the 1920s.*

5. *How does the play speak to the struggle of the individual versus larger society? What message does it contain about the power of the individual to change society?*

6. *Outline the various techniques Drummond uses over the course of the trial to undermine Brady's literal interpretation of the Bible. How does Drummond finally humiliate his opponent?*

REVIEW & RESOURCES

QUIZ

1. Why is Cates arrested?

    A. He is revealed to be a communist spy
    B. He clones a monkey and transforms it into a human
    C. He teaches high school students the theory of evolution
    D. The police suspect him in the murder of Tommy
        Stebbins

2. Who represents the prosecution in the play?

    A. Henry Drummond
    B. William Jennings Bryan
    C. Matthew Harrison Brady
    D. E. K. Hornbeck

3. What biologist's research and ideas led to what we know as
    the theory of evolution?

    A. James Watson
    B. Albert Einstein
    C. Gregor Mendel
    D. Charles Darwin

4. How does Howard offend Melinda in the first scene?

    A. He calls her father a monkey
    B. He swears
    C. He makes fun of the president
    D. He questions U.S. involvement in World War I

5. During what time of year does the trial take place?

    A. Spring
    B. Summer
    C. Fall
    D. Winter

6. Why does Rachel testify against Cates?

   A. Brady tricks her into thinking that Cates double-crossed her
   B. Her father forces her to
   C. She opposes evolution theory
   D. Brady seduces her

7. What happens when Brady arrives in Hillsboro?

   A. The town children take him on a hayride
   B. The townspeople greet him with great enthusiasm
   C. He experiences temporary amnesia
   D. He wins a fistfight with E. K. Hornbeck

8. What does the banner hanging in the center of town say?

   A. "Read Your Bible!"
   B. "Read Your Darwin!"
   C. "Welcome President Brady!"
   D. "Happy Fourth of July!"

9. What title does the judge use to address Brady?

   A. Counselor Brady
   B. Private Brady
   C. Senator Brady
   D. Colonel Brady

10. What is Drummond's reaction to Brady's title?

   A. He is glad Brady has finally won the proper recognition
   B. He feels intensely jealous
   C. He thinks it is ridiculous but wins the same title for himself
   D. He thinks Brady would make a better admiral

11. What does Drummond say in response to Cates's description of the townspeople's treatment of him?

   A. He has no idea what it must be like
   B. He shares the townspeople's view of Cates
   C. He has been in the same position
   D. He thinks Cates should try to win back the townspeople's approval by lying about his views

12. When did Rachel start to fear her father?

    A. When he beat her for the first time
    B. When he expressed his opposition to Cates
    C. When he said that Tommy Stebbins was condemned
    D. She has feared him from a very young age

13. What does Hornbeck do when Brady holds an informal press conference?

    A. He takes no notes and acts indifferently
    B. He eagerly scrambles down Brady's every word
    C. He yells at Brady despite the other reporters' efforts to silence him
    D. He translates Brady's words into the Hillsboro dialect

14. Which biblical story does Reverend Brown recite during his town prayer meeting?

    A. Jonah and the whale
    B. Creation
    C. The birth of Jesus
    D. Daniel in the lions' den

15. Why does Reverend Brown condemn his own daughter's soul to anguish?

    A. Because she has had a relationship with her cousin
    B. Because she supports Cates
    C. Because she has read *On the Origin of Species*
    D. Because she believes in D. H. Lawrence

16. What real-life court case provided the inspiration for *Inherit the Wind*?

    A. *McCulloch v. Maryland*
    B. *Dartmouth College v. Woodward*
    C. *Tennessee v. John Thomas Scopes*
    D. *Brown v. Board of Education*

REVIEW & RESOURCES

17. How do Rachel and Cates know each other?

    A.   They attend the same church
    B.   They are cousins
    C.   They teach at the same school
    D.   Their fathers are friends

18. Who is Tommy Stebbins?

    A.   A local boy who drowned
    B.   Cates's illegitimate son
    C.   Reverend Brown's assistant
    D.   One of Brady's henchmen

19. Why is Rachel dismissed from the witness stand?

    A.   She has provided all the necessary answers
    B.   She appears pale and ill
    C.   She refuses to swear on the Bible
    D.   She acts violently

20. What unusual and unexpected courtroom maneuver does Drummond make?

    A.   Calling evolutionist experts to the stand
    B.   Calling Brady to the stand
    C.   Calling a thirteen-year-old to the stand
    D.   Calling no one to the stand

21. What is the significance of the radio man's presence at the trial?

    A.   He has just invented the radio and is testing it in Hillsboro
    B.   This is the first time a trial has been broadcast on the radio
    C.   The Hillsboro townspeople have never heard radio before
    D.   The radio man gets into a fight with Hornbeck about journalistic integrity

22. What is Cates's sentence?

    A.   A $100 fine
    B.   A $10,000 fine
    C.   Ten years in jail
    D.   One year in jail

23. What does Brady recite in his delirium after he becomes ill?

    A.   The speech he had prepared for his presidential victory
    B.   Passages from *On the Origin of Species*
    C.   The Sermon on the Mount
    D.   The Pledge of Allegiance

24. How does Brady die?

    A.   Brain damage
    B.   Consumption
    C.   A heart attack
    D.   A busted belly

25. Which pair of characters leaves together on the evening train?

    A.   Drummond and District Attorney Davenport
    B.   E. K. Hornbeck and Melinda
    C.   Howard and Melinda
    D.   Rachel and Cates

SUGGESTIONS FOR FURTHER READING

CHAPMAN, MATTHEW. *Trials of the Monkey: An Accidental Memoir.* London: Duck Editions, 2000.

CONKIN, PAUL KEITH. *When All the Gods Trembled: Darwinism, Scopes, and American Intellectuals.* Lanham, Maryland: Rowman and Littlefield Publishers, 1998.

COUCH, NENA. "An Interview with Jerome Lawrence and Robert E. Lee." *Studies in American Drama, 1945–Present.* Vol. 7, 1992. 3–18.

DARWIN, CHARLES. *On the Origin of Species by Means of Natural Selection.* New York: Bantam Classics, 1999.

DE CAMP, L. SPRAGUE. *The Great Monkey Trial.* Garden City, New York: Doubleday, 1968.

GINGER, RAY. *Six Days or Forever: Tennessee v. John Thomas Scopes.* Boston: Beacon Press, 1958.

LARSON, EDWARD J. *Summer for the Gods: The Scopes Trial and America's Continuing Debate over Science and Religion.* Cambridge, Massachusetts: Harvard University Press, 1998.

SCOPES, JOHN THOMAS. *Center of the Storm: Memoirs of John T. Scopes.* New York: Holt, Rinehart and Winston, 1967.

TEACHOUT, TERRY. *The Skeptic: A Life of H. L. Mencken.* New York: HarperCollins, 2002.

REVIEW & RESOURCES